★
THE
**BIG** TIME

# ALBERT PUJOLS

AARON FRISCH

CREATIVE 🍎 EDUCATION

# ALBERT PUJOLS

## TABLE OF CONTENTS

# MEET ALBERT

Albert waits at the plate. The pitcher throws a hard fastball. But it is not fast enough to get past Albert! He swings and hits it. The crowd goes wild as the ball flies into the stands for a home run.

Albert Pujols (*POO-holz*) is a star baseball player for the Los Angeles Angels of Anaheim. He is a powerful ***slugger*** and a great first baseman. Many people think Albert is the best player in baseball today.

*Albert has won baseball awards for both his hitting and his fielding*

# ALBERT'S CHILDHOOD

**A**lbert was born January 16, 1980, in Santo Domingo. That is the *capital* of the Dominican Republic. Albert's grandmother helped to raise him. The Pujols family was poor, but Albert was happy.

*Kids in the Dominican Republic*

**SANTO DOMINGO, DOMINICAN REPUBLIC**

# GETTING INTO BASEBALL

**A**s a boy, Albert played baseball almost every day. When he was 16, Albert moved to the United States with some of his family. They lived in Independence, Missouri.

*Thousands of people in Missouri became Albert Pujols fans*

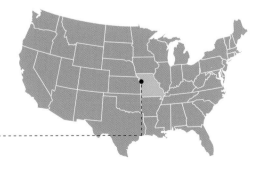

**INDEPENDENCE, MISSOURI**

At first, Albert spoke only Spanish. But in high school, he learned English. He became a baseball star, too. He was strong and could smash long home runs. Albert dreamed of playing major-league baseball.

*In Spanish, a home run might be called a "jonrón"* (HONE-RONE)

# THE BIG TIME

In 1999, the St. Louis Cardinals **drafted** Albert. He played in the minor leagues for one year and then joined the Cardinals. As a **rookie**, Albert hit 37 home runs! But he cared more about his team than he did about himself.

........................................................

*Albert played for the Potomac Cannons team (in Virginia) in the minor leagues in 1999*

For the next 10 seasons, Albert helped make the Cardinals a great team. He hit 445 total homers and hardly ever struck out. With their big first baseman, the Cardinals won the World Series in 2006 and 2011.

................................................

*In 2011, St. Louis won its 11th World Series*

# OFF THE FIELD

**A**lbert is married and has four kids. When he is not playing baseball, he spends most of his time at home. Albert is religious and goes to church regularly. He also likes to work out to stay in good shape.

*The oldest of Albert's two boys is named Albert Jr.*

# WHAT IS NEXT?

In 2011, Albert changed teams. He joined the Los Angeles Angels of Anaheim for $254 million! Albert hopes his mighty swing will help his new team win the World Series in the seasons ahead.

*Albert became one of the biggest sports stars in Los Angeles when he joined the Angels*

# WHAT ALBERT SAYS ABOUT ...

## HIS FAMILY

"I try to spend as much time as possible with God and my family. That's more important than anything I'm doing in baseball."

## HITTING A BASEBALL

"I try to see the ball and have a plan. That's how you become a good hitter, when you tell yourself what you're doing wrong and correct it the next at bat."

## WORKING HARD

"You know, if you work hard, your hard work is going to pay off one day."

## GLOSSARY

**capital** a city that is the main center for something

**drafted** picked to be on a team; in a sports draft, teams take turns choosing players

**rookie** a player in his first season

**slugger** a baseball player who can hit the ball very hard

## READ MORE

Mattern, Joanne. *Albert Pujols*. Mankato, Minn.: Capstone, 2011.

Monnig, Alex. *Albert Pujols: Groundbreaking Slugger*. Minneapolis: Abdo, 2012.

## WEB SITES

### Angels Kids
*http://losangeles.angels.mlb.com/ana/ fan_forum/kids_index.jsp*
This is the Web site of Albert's team, the Los Angeles Angels of Anaheim.

### Baseball Reference
*http://www.baseball-reference.com/players/p/ pujolal01.shtml*
This page lists Albert's statistics and all the honors he has won.

## INDEX

**PUBLISHED BY** Creative Education
P.O. Box 227, Mankato, Minnesota 56002
Creative Education is an imprint of The Creative Company
www.thecreativecompany.us

**DESIGN AND PRODUCTION BY** Christine Vanderbeek
**ART DIRECTION BY** Rita Marshall
**PRINTED IN** the United States of America

**PHOTOGRAPHS BY** Alamy (EPA European Pressphoto Agency B.V.), Dreamstime (Aspenphoto), Getty Images (Diamond Images, Jeff Gross, Harry How, John Iacono/Sports Illustrated, Ronald C. Modra/Sports Imagery, Layne Murdoch, Ezra Shaw, Rob Tringali/Sportschrome, Josh Umphrey, Tim Umphrey, Dilip Vishwanat), iStockphoto (Edward Grajeda, Pingebat), Shutterstock (George Dolgikh, Alex Staroseltsev)

**LIBRARY OF CONGRESS CATALOGING-IN-PUBLICATION DATA**
Frisch, Aaron.
Albert Pujols / Aaron Frisch.
p. cm. — (The big time)
Includes bibliographical references and index.
*Summary:* An elementary introduction to the life, work, and popularity of Albert Pujols, a professional baseball star who played first base and helped the St. Louis Cardinals win two World Series.

**ISBN 978-1-60818-336-4**
1. Pujols, Albert, 1980-—Juvenile literature. 2. Baseball players—Dominican Republic—Biography—Juvenile literature. I. Title.
GV865.P85F75 2013
796.357092—dc23 [B] 2012013476

First edition
9 8 7 6 5 4 3 2 1